MW01053931

Bedrooms

Bedrooms

Kim Waller

AND THE EDITORS OF

Victoria MAGAZINE

HEARST BOOKS • A DIVISION OF STERLING PUBLISHING CO., INC. • NEW YORK

Copyright © 1998 by Hearst Communications, Inc.

All rights reserved.

Produced by Smallwood & Stewart Inc., New York City
Edited by Carrie Chase
Designed by Patti Ratchford

Library of Congress Cataloging-in-Publication Data
Available upon request.

10 9 8 7 6 5 4 3 2 1

Published by Hearst Books,
A Division of Sterling Publishing Co., Inc.
387 Park Avenue South, New York, N.Y. 10016

Victoria and Hearst Books are trademarks owned by
Hearst Magazines Property, Inc., in USA,
 and Hearst Communications, Inc., in Canada.

www.victoriamag.com

Distributed in Canada by Sterling Publishing
C/o Canadian Manda Group, One Atlantic Avenue, Suite 105
Toronto, Ontario, Canada M6K 3E7
Distributed in Australia by Capricorn Link (Australia) Pty. Ltd.
P.O. Box 704, Windsor, NSW 2756 Australia

Manufactured in China

ISBN 1-58816-192-7

Contents

Foreword

hese things I love—crisp sheets scented as if just from the line, morning light to awaken me to the hope of a new day, handmade quilts so comfy I rest easily—and all are among the joys of my bedroom. For me, as for so many of us, my bedroom is where private reverie refreshes and nourishes me. My reading chair is just at the right angle and I can reach exactly an arm's length for my tea and my glasses. Here, I have things as I choose. And sometimes that includes stacks of books waiting to be read and pictures resting against the wall until I find the moment to hang them.

Ever since *Victoria* began we have had a mission about encouraging people to create places of intimacy in their homes. With this book, we have gathered decorating ideas along with inspirations for making your bedroom the sanctuary you deserve. Here you can indulge yourself in a fairy-tale four-poster, put out the treasure closest to your heart, and have luxury at your fingertips. Guests, too, love to stay in rooms that welcome them with your own specialness. You'll find lovely ideas here to do just that.

Morning song is most beautiful, and evening comes nigh with eloquence in the private world you create. We hope this book helps bring you these pleasures.

NANCY LINDEMEYER
Founding Editor
Victoria Magazine

Introduction

More than any room in our lives, the bedroom is a place apart. It is here that we invite our dreams and renew our energies, closing the door gently on the day's obligations to remember our own needs, our essential selves. As the great shadow of night rolls across half the world, dividing light from dark, so the bedroom, to which we retire as a bird to its bough, divides our private life from our public one. Whatever we are to others, in the bedroom we are our own person, folding down a coverlet, plumping a pillow, opening a book.

Though from ancient times the hearth has been the symbol of home, a case could be made today that the bedroom is just as meaningful an image. If home is about sanctuary and shelter, then the bedroom is its ultimate expression, the very heart of the matter. We entrust one-third of the hours of our lives to its embrace. It is here we renew the joys and intimacies of marriage, nuzzle our newborn infants close, and open our eyes to each new morning. From childhood on, we turn to "our room" to be comforted—not only by snuggling with a sigh under an aptly named comforter, but also by surrounding ourselves with meaningful objects and pictures, soothing fabrics, and family mementoes that delight and console.

The comforts are as various as the styles that suit us. To some, a room without flowers—dancing on curtains or coverlets or nestled in a bedside vase—is like a day without sunshine. Others seek repose in only the simplest of surroundings, the calmest of colors. Yet another wants happy pursuits at hand: piles of good books, or one's own needlepoint creations, or a desk whose cubbies overflow with sketches, shells, and pinecones.

The truth is that many of us find our way slowly in the process of fashioning a true retreat. One day we want the mood romantic; the next, cozy. And why shouldn't a bedroom, of all places, be accommodating to our whims? As the most personal of spaces, it changes with us, is flexible to fancy and fun to renew.

As *Victoria* welcomes you into bedrooms we have loved and admired, we hope you will find inspiration for your own sanctuary on these pages. And we hope you enjoy the wide view we take, offering restful retreats for your family and friends as well, and even a tempting corner or two for a little afternoon nap.

Sleep's Chamber

PART ONE

Grand and Humble

Down the hall or under the eaves, perhaps in its own separate wing, the bedroom in this century has been a paean to privacy—an ideal built not only into our American Constitution but into our very homes. Yet, surprisingly enough, privacy is rather a latecomer to the world's domestic arrangements. When darkness fell of a winter's eve in the Middle Ages, most families pulled pallets stuffed with straw close to the fire in the one main room used for cooking and living, then bundled them away at daylight, perhaps shooing aside the animals who shared their roof. Even travelers stopping at a roadside inn could expect to share the bedcovers with strangers. In the democracy of sleep, warmth was what mattered.

Once, such a handsome four-poster might have been entirely curtained in heavy drapes, for many people believed that night air bore contagion on its dark wings. But by the mid-19th century, the cry changed to: "Away with dusty bed curtains! In with healthy fresh air!" And down they came, leaving but a panel or two to stir in the new decorative breezes.

The nobles of the Renaissance, equally subject to chilly drafts, slept more cozily, if stuffily, in a high-framed bed curtained all about with sumptuous woven and embroidered fabrics. Often placed in the center of a chamber, the bed was like an enclosed room within a room within a house, its draperies, when dropped, offering seclusion for pillow talk. Perhaps the most opulent such bedrooms the world has seen were created for France's 17th- and 18th-century monarchs, who lavished all the artistry of the realm on their vast, jewellike palaces. While humbler folk still curled under homespun in a chimney alcove, Marie Antoinette slept beneath a soaring canopy of carved and gilded cupids, swathed in gorgeously embroidered silk; at

Versailles, Louis XIV snoozed within magnificent floor-to-ceiling drapes of gold-thread brocade. Yet even his bedroom was not private: Daily, the entire court trooped in to wake him!

Though by the 18th century many an affluent couple could retire to sleeping and dressing rooms apart from the household hubbub (sometimes separate ones for master and mistress; hence "master bedroom"), it wasn't until the 19th century that bedrooms became universal in ordinary homes, a place deemed necessary for domestic happiness and healthy sleep.

A goose down featherbed, a quilt, perhaps a long-handled bedwarmer—such comforts were cherished, for women spent many hours of their lives here, recuperating from childbirth, visiting with friends, or knitting by the fire while keeping watch

A canopied bed lends height and majesty to an artist's apartment in Charleston, South Carolina. Living above the gallery she runs is no hardship for the artist, whose apartment reflects her passion for beauty, color, and tradition. To extend the vista of her living room, she need only draw back the drapes that, instead of a door, separate off her bedroom. And when she does so, suddenly the antique four-poster, a family heirloom, becomes part of the room's sense of heritage.

Even her paintings of chairs flanking the pilasters express a love for antiques. Charleston's gentle neoclassicism is here, too— in symmetrical pairs of painted cabinets and matching armchairs by the sofa—but the artist plays the past her own way, right down to an informal straw rug. As in a lady's bedchamber–sitting room of long ago, friends, artists, and clients often gather here, the scene of a social life on which the grand bed looks on, unabashed.

In the same Charleston apartment, the artist gathers together a veritable still-life of heirlooms and family photos on her writing desk and vanity. And though you might think these beloved objects have pushed real work entirely off the desk, this is not the case here: For the flowers in the vase, or the antique figurine on the lamp, opposite, might at any moment become part of a new painting, such as the one just glimpsed on the wall. Not only do the images of generations of a family that cared for lovely things come together on the vanity, right, but so too do luxurious textures—silver, porcelain, crystal, and alabaster. "Interiors fascinate me," says the owner, "because they reveal so much about one's life philosophy."

over a sick child. In fact, in early American homes, where parlor seating was uncomfortably stiff-backed, the only restful, upholstered chair in the house could be found in the main bedroom or that of an aged parent: often a horsehair-padded wing chair, known as "an invalid chair," pulled close to the hearth. And it's still a lovely idea.

Though the bedroom has certainly been sensitive to the winds of fashion, its promise remains delightfully constant: repose in privacy. Today the room where we are freest is also one we are free to reinvent, happily mixing new design with beauty borrowed from other ages.

GOOSE DOWN

A flock of geese strutting about the farmyard was often a good indication that those within slept well, for in early America a feather bed—finer than a straw or hair mattress—was "deemed essential for comfortable people," wrote a Connecticut gentleman. Even though the poor, squawking geese were plucked three times a year, it took a long time for a householder to accumulate the forty pounds of feathers required for a proper feather bed. Eventually, commercial outlets began to supply the stuffing. Today we are more likely to sleep under than over the down, which is not always of the fluffiest goose: duck and even chicken feathers are also enlisted. But the label is sure to declare which creature contributed to your sybaritic sense of sleeping in a cloud.

I n winter, the sensation of bare toes sprinting across cold floor-boards is all the basic science one needs to explain why our forebears favored high beds. As the cold air settled, the sleeper rose, often requiring the help of steps, to a bed—perhaps a handsome Federal four-poster—which would be mounded in the middle with an eiderdown. One Massachusetts girl worried that "unless I landed exactly in the centre of the mountainous island . . . I passed my night rolling downhill, or in vain efforts to scramble up to the top, to avoid falling out on the floor." Now honored in a restored Pennsylvania farmhouse, this antique bed is lavished with pillows of tapestry and lace, vintage linen skirts—and a perfectly contemporary down quilt. The bedroom's pier glass, pictures, and wing chairs recall the finery of those chillier chambers of old.

A Quiet Retreat

As our lives grow busier and the world noisier, the bedroom, that quiet space we call our own, becomes more important than ever. Honoring it is like honoring ourselves, less an indulgence than a necessity. Certainly, some of the most delicious hours of life are bedroom hours—reading to a sleepy child, stroking a tentative kitten, dressing for an important evening, spreading out the Sunday papers. Simply curling up alone with a cup of tea can be a declared holiday, our time out of time. And even if there is no soft-footed maid to carry a tray to the bedside, and we do it ourselves, is the moment any the less perfect? Maybe more so. For getting out of bed only to climb right back in may be life's most satisfying activity.

What a pleasure to just lie back and listen. We hear the lively titter of chickadees at the bird-feeder outside, the jeer of a jay. We hear the rustle of a down comforter as we roll over, or the consoling patter of rain against the window. Most of all, we can listen to our own thoughts, letting the mind wander through back roads far from the day's speeding highway.

Most of us would admit we touch up the living room and dining room with an eye to how they will appear to others. What we ask of a bedrooom is something different—that it reach out and touch us. We want fabrics soft as a mother's caress and mementoes meaningful to ourselves alone. The bedroom that satisfies both body and soul is a place where we can reach beyond ourselves, because here, in quiet, we are most ourselves.

A rainy Sunday, when all the world seems somnolent, can come as a gentle gift, a yawn in time. That's when you can instruct the family that people who nap live longer, and retire guiltlessly to practice what you preach. And it's true: In the softness of pillows, one finds renewed optimism and strength.

One merry print does wonders in creating a delightful bedroom suite at the top of the house, where sisters can whisper late into the night. Like Meg and Jo in "Little Women," who also shared a garret bedroom, the residents are removed from the tramp and tumult of the household. It's hard to believe this space was originally an undistinguished catchall, long and narrow with small windows and rough walls. But a toile de Jouy print brings the space to life with French charm. The documentary print, wrapping walls, ceilings, and even windows, and celebrating the 18th-century balloon ascent of the brothers Montgolfier, is a favorite French motif. Given the subject, the balloon curtains at the window seem fitting. A beautiful surprise: wrought-iron gates used as headboards. A cozy adjoining area, opposite, with sofa and floral pillows, makes this aerie a complete retreat.

"Dark walls are wonderful for setting off framed art," says the owner of this small Victorian townhouse. Such warm colors can also make a glowing nest of a modestly sized bedroom, almost filled by a splendid 19th-century bed from the island of Majorca. Where space is limited, everything that meets the eye counts for more. A few treasures—fine engravings, a piece of antique embroidery on the cheerful basket pillow—are enough to give a satisfying sense of elegance and individuality. And when the vintage chintz drapes, with their pattern of grapes, are drawn against city lights and the sound of traffic, this small world of peace is exquisitely self-contained.

"A little warmth, a little light
Of love's bestowing—and so, good night."

GEORGE LOUIS PALMELLA BUSSON DU MAURIER

There's a general rule that says the bed should be centered on the longest bedroom wall. *Right* enough, in some cases. But when both corner windows look on the garden, who could resist spending a quiet morning merely turning one's head on the pillow to check the azaela's progress—or the comings and goings of a mother robin? The view is such an important part of a bedroom that we do well to let **it**, not the "rules," signal the most pleasurable placement of furniture. How fortunate we are when that view—whether of sunny fields or neighborly rooftops—composes an image of life we never tire of. Then, belled with a bow, even the curtains can be persuaded to let in the glory of greenery crowding the panes.

The Bed Beautiful

As we slip gratefully under the covers at day's end, we are one with all who ever lived, and grew weary, and slept. Sooner or later, we must abed. As central to our lives as to our homes, the bed is an arena of profound human experience. For many of our forebears, the gates of life opened and closed upon the very same family bed. Others, wanderers from Bedouins to soldiers to cowboys, carried their bedding with them, and it was home to them on whatever ground. Rather fussier about her nocturnal arrangements, one young lady proved herself a fairy-tale princess by being unable to sleep upon a pea, even atop twenty mattresses and twenty featherbeds. In literature, perhaps the most moving of all beds was the most difficult to move. The stalwart bed of Odysseus, symbol of a firm marriage that endured the hardship of a long separation, was carved from a single, deep-rooted tree trunk—a secret known only to the man and wife who cherished it.

As passion's playground and fever's solace, our bed is the ultimate safe place, where we turn to be mended, loved, and soothed. But it has also been a statement of pride and fashion, soaring to regal heights, adorned with fabulous carvings intended to impress. It has been shaped as an oval, a boat, a sleigh, built as a cozy cabinet, stacked in bunks, or laid simply upon the floor. It has been as skinny as a camp cot and capacious as the Great Bed of Ware, which supposedly measured 12 by 18 feet (fitted sheets not available), and was quite an

In her grandfather's house in South Berwick, Maine, author Sarah Orne Jewett lived for many productive years with her sister, Mary, who at Sarah's insistence had the "best" bedroom. The knotted and tassled canopy over a domed frame must have been shaped for this bed alone. The knitted coverlet is a masterwork of skill.

We have the Romans to thank for adding a headboard and footboard to the Greek's couch-like bed. Since most meals were eaten while the diner reclined, the headboard—not always inlaid with jewels like Nero's, but certainly lavished with silken pillows—made lounging all the more languorous and infinitely easier on the elbows. It's a truth anyone sitting up for a cup of soup after an illness can vouch for. And what is breakfast in bed without a firm backrest? (Ironically, breakfast was one meal the Romans often ate standing up.) Opposite: The headboard here, reminiscent of carved oak wall paneling, would be quite at home in a stately English manor house, though the hills of puffy pillows make one long to try dining Roman-style—stretching out a hand for a grape and a goblet. Right: Pencil-thin bed posts, airy yet architectural, barely etch a restful nook. This high frame is draped in the simplest manner possible: just lengths of net looped casually over the corner finials.

attraction at the 16th-century inn that held it. From the Middle Ages on, a handsomely crafted bed became an important family heirloom—which leaves one wondering why Shakespeare bequeathed only his "second-best bed" to his wife.

The bed you choose will suggest the mood and style of the bedroom—spare or formal, casual or fanciful. Today simplicity and charm may speak more intimately to us than high glamour, yet designs that have pleased through the ages are still evoked and reinvented. Choose your boat of dreams with the heart, for it will carry you far and last for years, perhaps for generations.

Sometimes a very small bedroom can be even more enchanting than a large one. This Swedish-style nook makes a virtue of necessity by focusing loving attention on the upholstered bed, half-tented with a simple drape. With a puppy pillow for whimsey, a lacy knit coverlet for luxury, and a bedside chair for a tea cup, who would not be utterly content?

TWIG BEDS

The rustic style of a bent twig bed never fails to evoke the mists rising from a mountain lake at dawn, or the evening cry of a loon. Yet, surprisingly, this back-to-nature style took its impetus from the late 19th-century barons of industry who, to escape their throbbing factories and mills, built handsome log "great camps" on the wild Adirondack lakeshores. When the owners departed and ice sealed the lakes, handy caretakers spent the winter constructing amazing stick furnishings that seemed to have just stepped in from the deep woods. Today artisans from the Adirondacks to North Carolina carry on the tradition of crafting these one-of-a-kind pieces, each a unique collaboration between art and sapling.

Nymphs of the forest seem to have woven this rustic bed of arching hickory twigs—ideal for a midsummer night's dream. In fact, however, a Hollywood film producer commissioned the piece from an Ozark craftsman—one who skillfully coaxed the natural shape of his materials into rhythmic forms more frequently seen in iron or brass. Such is the delicacy of the twig work that it cages, rather than supports, the modern box spring and mattress within. This sylvan fantasy is hardly what one expects to find in trend-setting Hollywood, but after a long day given to meetings and decisions, the owner finds respite in surrounding herself with things beautifully made by hand. A haunter of flea markets, she has crowded her bedroom walls with mirrors of all shapes and sizes, including handpainted Victorian "vanity" mirrors over the bed, and on the wall. Prettily decorated, they permitted a lady to arrange her hair or hat while seeming to be merely studying the art.

Certain shapes have an appeal that makes them seem just short of eternal, and the sleigh bed is one. Though any child might love to imagine "dashing through the snow" in his bed, the gracefully balanced S-curves were a mark of ancient Greek furnishings long before Napoleon slept in a bed with a similar sweep. In the mid-19th century, it would have been made of polished mahogany for a fine home, and copied for cottagers in a simpler or painted wood. But time plays tricks and swaps with fashion: Today the painted versions, like this honey-toned bed with its original blithe bouquet, hold a special charm—prompting collectors to prowl back-road antiques shops, and contemporary craftspeople to revive the art of handpainted furniture. Fortunately, we can count on newer beds to adhere to standard sizes, a convenience that didn't really settle in until earlier in this century.

"Beds . . . allow more room for fanciful design and the stamp of personal taste than any other single piece of furniture."

MARK HAMPTON

A stately four-poster, at left, was once a tree—or trees. Following the dictates of tradition, the craftsman who turned, smoothed, joined, and stained its four tall masts worked in a time-honored vernacular rich with associations, ones the owners clearly honor. But when the artisan is also an artist, the very idea of a bed gets thrown in the air and reinvented. One contemporary "headboard," opposite, is a forest, a tracery of metal leaves that seem to have grown right out of the bedroom floor. In a room sparsely ornamented (save for an elfin bench where Tinkerbell might pause), the bed is sculpture one can sleep in, a delicate evocation of the thicket of dreams. Or, perhaps, of the very real trees from which beds have been hewn and shaped for centuries.

Nowadays, many of us start out with a mattress and box spring set on an iron frame, willing to wait awhile until we can afford the real bed of our dreams. Others find the lightness and simplicity of a bed without headboard or footboard exactly to their liking. The owner of this cottage had in fact been searching ("without much luck," she admits) for a bed that would suit her summery, relaxed style when she came across a weather-worn garden trellis with a shapely curve—and solved her problem in one serendipitous stroke. Mounted on the wall, her illusory headboard is art and architecture in one. Artificial roses in graded sizes, echoed on embroidered pillows, lend a sense of rose-cottage romance. Her suggestion: "If you can't find it, create it!"

We've all dreamed of it—to rest
our head under a bower of blossoms
and trailing vines, and sleep, like
a princess in a fairy-tale
illustration, amid petals and
perfumed breezes. What else are
the happy florals of our bedrooms
about? Giving free rein to fantasy,
a California floral designer
transformed a Victorian bedroom,
opposite, into a wonderland of
blossoms, garlanding a heavy
headboard with trailing jasmine
and ivy, and even tucking in a
bird's nest. Though few of us have
the resources that were lavished on
this floral festival in a historic
mansion, vines and tall trees that
flourish indoors can play a
delightful role in greening our
place of dreams. For a lasting
sense of fancy, a graceful
brass-and-iron bed, right, wears an
airy crown of silk flowers twined
with leaves.

SIGNATURE PIECE

One dominant piece can set the tone and feel for an entire room.

A fine antique of noble proportions, like a tall, glass-fronted secretary desk, would ordinarily command an important wall of the living room or study. Yet its presence in a paneled bedroom sets a stately tone for the whole chamber, a place for thoughtful hours amid treasured books. Any large piece, from a French armoire to a Chinese chest, can add unique distinction to the bedroom, and suggest other choices that will do it honor. Here, for example, an imposing headboard would seem extraneous; whereas the period chairs gathered around a simple tea table are as friendly, in their formal way, as gentleman chums of the same old school.

In a distinctive American style cherished from the Adirondacks to the Rockies and north to Montana, this warm-toned "rustic" bedroom is anything but frontier-rough, even though some of its materials are. A fireplace nook of beautiful stonework is cozily crowded with soft chairs and ottomans for a hearthside supper or reading on chilly nights. Essential to the mountain mood are colorful camp blankets woven with Indian motifs—one cleverly divided to serve as drapes—which seem born to companion birch bark and mellow wood walls. The room is a stylish tribute to our American romance with the wilderness, right down to its classic Hudson Bay blanket and accents of deep forest green.

Seasons and Signatures

PART TWO

Personal Expressions

Creativity, we know, is the child of sleep. How often does the answer to some difficult problem come to us, seemingly magically, as we wake up! Overnight, Rumplestilskin has woven our tangled straw into gold. Stories and maps, tapestries and tasks are given—sometimes barely whisked across the mind—by Morpheus, the Greek god of dreams, who apparently knows more about us than we do ourselves.

As the room where dream-thoughts and realities interpollinate, the bedroom is a natural place for us to explore our creative energies and interests. Here there is quiet—the other parent of creativity. A person who sketched on her homework as a child may set up her first easel in a corner where the light is clear and steady.

When morning light streams in, a bedroom corner devoted to gathering our thoughts can make all the difference to the day. On a simple writing desk, fabric for a decorating project reveals its true colors, and plans go forward. To honor the view, sheer curtains can be mounted to the side of the window frame.

A comfortable chair and table invites the knitter to spread out a pattern and choose her colors. In private, before the audience of the mirror, one can rehearse a speech or assemble an outfit. Even making space for the morning stretch-and-bend can help loosen the kinks and prepare us to climb the day's hill. And what a simple luxury it is to write letters in our slippers or snuggle into a bathrobe to converse with a journal!

Whether we mean it to happen or not, the bedroom tells our personal story. Special interests and beloved objects keep traipsing in after us like so many tag-along puppies. The bedside books mount. Someone empties shells from the seashore onto a windowsill and there they sit, polished by light. Those who must be surrounded

by growing things nestle more and more plants by the window, then echo them with botanical prints on the wall. Family photos hold a reunion on the desktop. And who would part with these talismans? For they are ourselves.

When an individual's delights and pursuits shape the spirit of a bedroom, it becomes more than a utilitarian space; it takes on the engaging warmth of personality. Furniture, for example, becomes more sociable when asked to accommodate a favorite collection—carved jade, or blue-and-white Jasperware, or handbound books, whatever the treasures one can't help compiling. Sometimes, as our eyes fall on them, these very objects can start drawing in the whole room, suggesting how the pale green of the jade could be picked up in a slipcover or pillow fabric; or the sky blue of a vase answered in a wallpaper pattern. Whatever the decorative hints that spring from one's interests, there's comfort in knowing they come, not from beyond one's life, but from its core.

Rather than ban what engages our waking hours, we are rewarded by giving it place amid a bedroom's many meanings. If a music stand—an object often beautiful in itself—rests open in a corner awaiting an hour of concentrated practice, the

A life crowded with projects and passions somehow makes room for it all, gathering artful containers the way a beach gathers shells. A long table with baskets of all shapes, opposite, helps organize those treasures we need to keep near us, always at hand to pore over in a quiet moment before sleep.

In a private chamber that also serves as an intimate sitting room, a woman of today, like her Edwardian counterpart, might spend a morning concentrating at her writing table, left, and later share confidences with a friend over sherry. Not so many decades ago, women would leave the men to their cigars and port after a dinner party and retire to the pleasures of their own talk by the fire. The fanlike French fire screen and lacquered tray-table, right, imply a subject of discussion—a recent shopping trip abroad.

whole room seems to listen. Near the window, a birdwatcher's guide, binoculars, and a life-list evoke the darting traffic of the sky. Even a flower that holds special meaning—the lilac, the violet, the rose—can encompass a room with patterns that, simply pretty to others, convey messages of joy to the sleeper.

Nowadays, more and more bedrooms do double duty as a home office, but the function is hardly new. Well before typewriters and computers, women sat at their bedroom desk to write thank-you notes, letters, even novels. To keep the emphasis on the home part of "home office," a handsome armoire or cabinet can be enlisted to keep files and papers in place. Under the skirts of a tall four-poster, one designer keeps her collection of fabric-swatch books tucked away until she needs them. Another shows all, filling the wall with watercolors of the rooms she is devising. And there they curl for a while, unframed, unfinished, like a sign that would serve for any creative woman's bedroom, saying: "Work in Progress Here."

READING BETWEEN THE COVERS

One of the great satisfactions of adulthood is not having to read under the covers with a flashlight. One can devour a whole novel until the wee hours, or just briefly skim an enticing cookbook and mark a few recipes before the eyelids droop. For many, settling down with a book before sleep is like a massage for the mind—it relaxes and stimulates at once, sweeping away the day's cares with pleasurable concentration and good company. Comfort is first: Firm support for the neck and back, and a lamp that illuminates the page, can make all the difference in finding out whodunnit. And if some half-read volume has lingered for months by the bedside without a glimpse, just firmly remove it. There's so much else to read—even a book about bedrooms!

Arranging a bedroom to suit our pursuits is a delightful challenge. This gardener spends her winter digging deep into horticultural tomes, seeking ideas to try next year, and keeping notes on varieties she'll send away for. Before she had a simple cabinet and desk space built to hold them, her garden books sprang up everywhere—except where she was. Now the covetable rose in a photo can be looked up immediately in growers' catalogs saved in the drawers—and the cutting is all but on its way. Such a built-in cabinet would serve a skilled knitter just as well, perhaps with subdivided sections for all her colored wools, and a shelf to hold patterns for creating new heirlooms.

The writer Virginia Woolf claimed she felt insecure when it came to decorating. But for writing, she knew her needs: solitude, and "a room of one's own." At Monk's House, a delightful country cottage in Sussex that she and her husband, Leonard, bought in 1919, Virginia took over a plain room, which eventually gathered objects of meaning. The fireplace tiles were painted by her sister Vanessa Bell; the pictures were by another member of their Bloomsbury group. Although Virginia daily traipsed across the garden to write in a small shack, others of genius preferred to work propped on their pillows. Milton, Voltaire, Swift, George Sand, Elizabeth Barrett Browning, and Mark Twain all penned their quick thoughts in bed, and Puccini wrote some of his warmest arias while under the covers.

A ballet dancer's room nimbly accommodates her art as well as her need for rest. One long mirrored wall (overleaf) defines a home studio where she can stretch at the barre in toe shoes, perfecting the arc of an arm, the line of a leg. Light-limbed furniture, opposite, echoes that grace: An iron bed barely gestures at solidity, its texture and curve repeated in the metal desk chair. Though not a large room for such various functions, it seems airy and uncrowded, for the dancer has positioned the bed at a diagonal and let the narrow desk act as a semi-divider beween studio and bedroom. Soothing hues, with no distracting patterns, maximize light reflected in the studio mirror. The reward for such hard-working muscles: repose amid deep pillows, right.

Filled with exotic palms, a plant-lover's room holds winter at bay with its rich interplay of woven and printed leaf patterns. Like the Victorians, who built elegant glass-walled conservatories to showcase their botanical prizes, this connoisseur keeps nature ever green and gay. As real fronds nod from their antique pedestals, opposite, the paisley-like swirls on fabric hung like a wall tapestry are answered in the rug and bed throw. Layering compatible patterns in this careful way creates not only opulence but energy in a small space. Though the chair is covered in vintage fabric, contemporary prints dance across the bed pillows, left, confirming our endless fascination with the exuberant world of plants.

For an artist, every day is the dawn of creation, and light is its first word. When brushes and pencils stand ready on a serviceable bedroom table, there's every chance of capturing the shell-pale colors of morning, or an image offered in dreams. This artist's style—pastels that delight in an honest image—is suggested in her choice of simple furnishings and sun-washed cottons. A clarified mind, tuned to essentials, dwells here as easily as in any place inspiration beckons. Out the window, the glimpse of sea could be Normandy, or Maine, or Crete.

Summer Morning

Even before you open your eyes, you can breathe the morning news. That lime-sharp smell of fresh-cut grass—someone has been mowing. The breeze must be off the lake, you can taste it, and there's something else, sweet: Has the mock orange blossomed? Is it the lilies?

Like no other season, summer moves into the house through every open door and window, bringing with it sandy toes, bunches of roses, baskets of zucchini, and the neighbor's dog. Children in search of bathing towels and juice romp through and out as if the house were no more than a shelf in air. There is everything delicious to do, and no compunction to do it in a hurry.

With sun-dried sheets and curtains light as lingerie, the room where we wake to summer days takes the season's pleasures lightly. Particularly welcome are fabrics as easy on the eye as the skin: classic blue-and-white cottons, striped ticking, chenille or Marseilles spreads, prints with the freshness of a seaside garden. The days are too precious to spend in heavy housekeeping, so fabrics that launder well have the edge. In summer, our ancestors tied slipcovers over the velvet chairs and rolled up the serious rugs; and it's still a good idea. Rag rugs, sisal, even bare floors a broom can whisk clean are the order of the day. Like our favorite hot-weather meals—fresh, simple, and tasty—a bedroom lightened to essentials joins the liberation of summer, when the ideal decoration is a huge bowl of

Simple comforts suffice in a cottage by the sea. Why pack more than one sweater? Hung to dry on the screen, it's sure to be ready by evening. Like good campers, we're resourceful in summer, as is the best cottage furniture. This table, reminiscent of a Victorian washstand, can store anything —and is light enough to be moved wherever it's needed.

"White curtains softly and continually blown
As the free air moves quietly about the room..."

MAY SARTON

roadside wildflowers. Certain seasonal urges—to paint everything white, adopt farm kittens, and live exclusively on corn and butter—require second thoughts. But if the bedside table gathers silly novels and a few perfect shells, then there's all the more reason to linger here with a bun and a tea cup, laying no particular plans for the morning. Time itself seems to yawn and stretch as, beyond the window, trees sigh in their summer fullness. And besides, if you do linger a bit longer, perhaps someone else will have raked the grass cuttings.

The master bedroom in a family home exudes an air of gentle Southern tradition and orderly days. Over Sunday breakfast at the pedestal table, a couple can plan next week's events—perhaps a child's birthday, a garden-party luncheon, a night at the symphony. Creamy-white fabrics on dignified mahogany pieces and a pale sisal rug promise a cool morning, even as the summer sun mounts.

ummer romances are often the start of an enduring marriage, and the same can be said of those inseparable summer pals, blue and white. Like the sight of sails slicing heaven and sea, this happy pair never fails to lift our spirits. In the alchemy of design, leaves, roses, and peonies turn cobalt, sapphire, and baby blue, just as they have on plates and tea sets for centuries. By some breezy magic, blue-and-white fabrics always seem just-washed. This mix of compatible patterns can be tossed over a picnic table, hung at a window, draped on a daybed. In any situation, they're sure to make a happy marriage.

A person who is romantic at heart finds her own ways of making even a rented place reflect her personality. "Bring your own sheets," said the owners, and she's glad she did, for her blue roses and ruffled sham have brought femininity to a plain room, which now seems fresh and cool whatever the day's temperature.

There are never enough vacation days to crowd in everything we dream of doing—get out the water skis, have a picnic with old friends, explore the country antiques shops. And then one day it rains. Rain curtains the harbor and tiptoes over the wooden roof saying "hush now." And, at last, we do. It's a day to climb back into bed after lunch in a room whose bright rose print on curtains, quilt, and lampshade seems to hold its own sunlight, a day to sink into that novel there was never time enough to read. In such a room, timeless and cozy, one can finally be on vacation from vacation.

COTTON TICKING

Ticking stripes appeal for their unpretentious charm——just the mood we want in summer.

Peek under a cotton sheet at the tufted mattress or under the pillow slip at the pillow—and there's that good old striped cotton ticking holding everything together. The word ticking derives from the Latin "tika," meaning case, and the stuff has been around long enough to have once encased straw and horsehair as well as down. No wonder we're so nostalgic about ticking that we translate its clean patterns into cotton sheets, curtains, and crisp upholstery. Even a graceful French chair, the sort usually dressed in formal fabric, takes on a breezy air when seated with ticking, whose ruler lines set off the back's floral oval.

When a bedroom is off the porch, twilight brings the birds' sleepy calls, the sight of gulls winging home to their roost. And the thought of a nap—just a little one—before the dinner guests arrive becomes irresistible. On a painted iron bed, a type first used in hospitals in the 19th century and then adopted for cottages, bed linens of blue-and-white stripes have been summer favorites for man, woman, and child almost forever. Though they evoke old-fashioned mattress ticking to some, or a man's shirt to others, a fondness for stripes is simply as American as the flag.

On the bedside table and the vanity, above, the theme is smartly amplified in nautically striped lampshades.

"In the mountains, there you feel free."

T. S. Eliot

To escape the unhealthy heat of the cities, families and their servants once journeyed with trunk loads of silver and linens to mountain retreats, there to spin the summer away with picnics, tennis, and amateur theatricals. A young lady was deemed a "good sport" when she hiked with her swain and chums to a breathtaking outlook. Now as then, mountain nights are crisp, and tucking under a checked duvet, opposite, plumped over delicate, lace-edged sheets, promises sweet sleep. On a sleeping porch, left, a rough hickory bed becomes all softness when made up with a vintage dust ruffle and checked duvet.

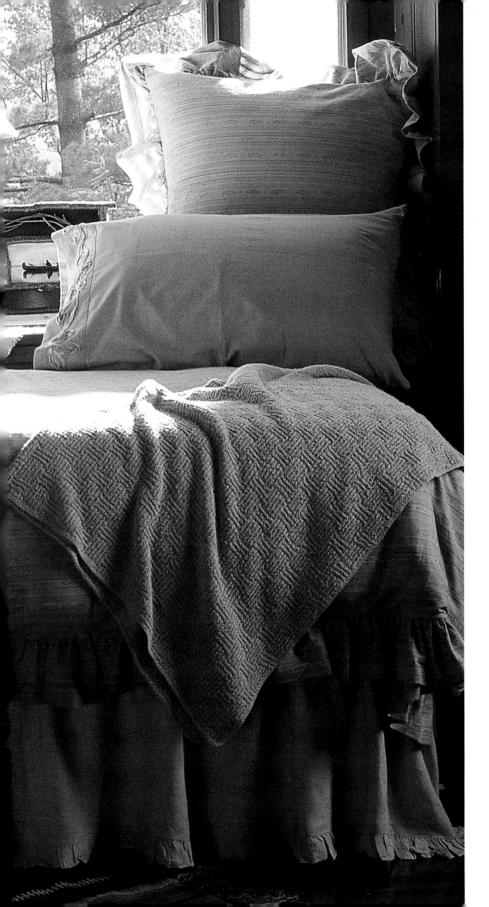

When the bedrooms overflow with company—the whole family up for a long weekend—being relegated to a living-room daybed overlooking the lake is no hardship. Propped on extra pillows and nestled in buttery flannel sheets, this sleeper reads late, and wakes early to catch dawn's first tinting of the still lake, where an early fisherman dips a rippling oar. A slatted chair from the patio is no fussier about where it is put: Drawn up to act as an impromptu table, it serves just as well indoors as out.

Winter Warmth

Few of us are as housebound in winter as our ancestors were, though sometimes we wish we might be. When wind scours the brown fields, when snow comes fast and keeps on coming, we exult in burrowing in for a fireside day of puzzles and popcorn. As long as there's an afghan to curl under, some soup, heat, and each other, we are happy to let the world retreat. The hours sift softly, snowflakes on a sill. When the snowplow finally clanks by, its flashing lights blurred in a spume of flung snow, there's relief—but a twinge of sadness, too, in knowing that everything, alas, is back to normal.

It is winter's gift to turn us inward. Now all that shelters and comforts us, or brightens the short days, comes forward to help us through. Lamplight, pictures—things we live with and forget to notice—seem more poignant in winter, like music listened to instead of merely heard. We crave color and company, hearty food, and deep sleep.

Winter may be the bedroom's ultimate season—as if some memory lingered of those long hibernal snoozes before mammals became humans. For now we love to surround ourselves with the finest of animal fabrics—wool and mohair, cashmere and down. Blanketing our homes in rich colors and Christmas reds is a way to defy nature's gray palette. Choosing creamy whites, we magnify the fleeting hours of light. And those who snooze under cotton-stuffed quilts are doubly comforted—by the thought of ancestors similarly warming their cold toes.

A quilt that's simplicity itself—no patches to pattern or assemble—can be easily made from two lengths of printed fabric. This contemporary one takes advantage of bands of stripes to show off alternating styles of machine stitching.

Every year we look forward to it—the inventive, puttering ritual of decking the house for Chistmastide. In come armloads of fresh-cut greens, out come the old ornaments, the chipped sheep and sleeping child for the crèche. There's so much delight in seeing the twinkling tree and front-door wreath that it's hard to stop there. This bedroom is given to whites most of the year, but at Christmas it, too, carols the season with shams of red schoolgirl plaid and a different plaid dust ruffle over its lace petticoat. The quilt gets a velvet duvet, and a trim of black skims the pillow, below. As the fire flickers, parents wrap late-night presents, their retreat already wrapped for the holidays.

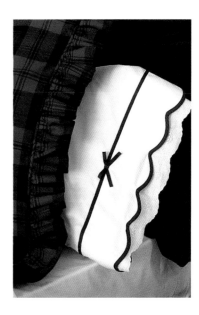

A ROOM AGLOW

Why should glorious candelabras be confined to the dining room alone? Does it take a stormy night and a power failure to bring the magic of candlelight into the bedroom? A nostalgic chamber, with floral rug and handpainted chests, seems made for the mystery of candlelight. Bring flowers, too, or fragrant candles, be bride and groom again in a room aglow. For hasn't fire been forever the symbol of love? Here are textures worthy of a candle's warm glance: damask sheets, crocheted throw, lacy dust ruffle, and sheer bed curtains loosely draped. In an old Victorian house, the white bed floats in reflections off the varnished wainscotting. Beauty, too, is a passion worth honoring. So light the candles, and let it snow.

In winter I get up by night / And dress by yellow candlelight," wrote Robert Louis Stevenson of those dawns before homes were illuminated with the flick of a switch. Ever since the mythic Prometheus stole fire from the gods to benefit man, we've confronted winter's darkness with every means possible—torches, whale oil, kerosene, gas lamps, all mercifully superannuated. But, ah, candles we keep, for there is such forgiveness and romance in their golden flickering, glinting off silver, sculpting a beloved face, that to light one or many is always something of a ritual, an act of confirmation.

WINTER WHITES

I f, one winter morning, you were
offered a bowl of light for
breakfast, what would it hold? The
colors of cream and honey and snow,
with here and there a pearly glint.
When a bedroom is fitted for winter
in such quiet hues, our eyes drink
in the sun's best effort the minute we
wake. The whites we love in winter
are warm whites, natural companions
to tea and toast and lamplight. Ivory
linen sheets on the bed grow only
softer with years of washing; with
the addition of a butter-pale print
or two, one's cup of morning is full.
On a luxurious chaise, opposite,
like a throne of leisure, a pillow
embroidered with pearls and a
supple throw of thick linen
suggest a comfortable alternative
to reading in bed.

"In the depth of winter, I finally learned that within me there lay an invincible summer."

ALBERT CAMUS

When an ice storm arrives to coat every twig and bent branch, the world outside is transformed into a crystal palace—a glitter and flashing almost too bright to look at! Clearly, this is a morning too treacherous for travel, so pull back the shantung drapes, left, and climb back into the pillows. On such a morning, a bedroom can be its own winter palace. On a tall bed, opposite, white-on-white sheets and shams of purest linen are never icy, especially when paired with rosy beige, like the antique coverlet of ribboned silk. The tea-stained chintz that slipcovers the bedside chair is equally cheering stitched as a dust ruffle—one that deliberately leaves the wood frame of the high bed exposed. As a breeze clatters through the frozen garden, dream that when you open your eyes again the roses will be in bloom.

The desire to surround ourselves with the cream of fabrics seems strongest in winter, when only the comforts of home stand between us and the nipping winds. Stamping indoors with tingling fingers after sledding with the children, we want nothing more than to sink into a deep chair and wrap our hands around a hot cup of cocoa. Not only does a mohair pillow, above, cosset with its silky fur, but, in a room of white accents, it offers a distinctive note of texture— as does the exquisitely hand-embroidered linen pillow opposite. Texture, in fact, is the real secret to combining winter whites. When played together in the key of white, wool chalet, a nubbly tweed, soft velvet, or gleaming damask fend off uniformity and lend a room the intricate intrigue of gloss and nap.

Since few houses today are finished with handsome interior moldings or paneling, one of the questions that bedevils homeowners is this: How to achieve some of the warmth of detail that marked well-made homes of the past? One answer is to add crown moldings to ceilings and strip molding to walls; another is simply to plunder the past for architectural and decorative elements that are not copies, but have been rescued—sometimes in odd-sized pieces—from an older house. Loving what the mellow glow of wood paneling can do for a room in a cold clime, these owners backed their bed with a section of library paneling found at auction, then added a draped tester to make this headwall more like a headboard. Rather than framed art, a wall tapestry completes the creative, stately-home mood.

Special Spaces

PART THREE

To Comfort a Guest

A home that hums with life, be it spacious or cozy, finds a way to make friends and overnight guests feel as cherished as family. What a luxury to be able to say "Oh, you must stay with us over the wedding weekend," or to know you can include an aunt or grandmother in the family festivities at holiday time, confident they'll be comfortable—however late the teenagers stay up. Those who love company but lack extra bedrooms often convert areas not intended for sleeping to the cause of hospitality. A favorite choice is the attic—which has its own charm and problems. Though dormers and larger windows can add light, it's often hot in summer: a good place for air conditioning. Even a sliver of a room—perhaps an old sewing room or study—makes a marvelous nest when fixed up with cheerful wallpaper and matching bed linens with pampering pillows. After all, it's comfort, privacy, and an accessible bath that make a guest feel at home and rested, not the proportions of the chamber. Though the guest room may not be the "best" room, a truly good bed and a well-placed reading lamp will always be appreciated.

Probably the most important ingredient of a guest room is empathy—knowing that what pleases and eases you will bring a smile to a traveler as well. Fresh flowers by the bed, a framed picture that includes your friend, a gift the person brought last time prominently displayed or used—these touches warm the heart as even the finest coverlet cannot. If

Traveling cases and steamer trunks piled at the end of the bed often did double duty as tables—especially in homes devoid of storage closets. Expecting a visit from her mother, one hostess put out mementoes that once adorned her grandmother's bureau—a welcome knit with family continuity and love.

the stay will be for several days, think of providing the convenience of a phone and perhaps an electric tea kettle, cup and saucer, tea bags, and a tin of homemade cookies. No visitor wants to trouble the hostess for little needs, so thoughtful provisions—a new toothbrush, a lovely soap and shampoo—can make all the difference in making a guest feel independent.

Decorating a guest room can often be more fun than doing up one's own—after all, there are fewer belongings one has to fit in. Here is the perfect setting for that pretty chest with small drawers, or the petite lady's desk that won't take the computer. Delicate or heirloom fabrics get light use here, and a piece or two of fine porcelain is out of the path of youngsters and leaping pets. In fact, just looking at a sweet guest room, all made up and ready, makes one want to lift the phone and say: "Do come for the weekend!"

The Victorians were inveterate travelers, climbing aboard carriages, steamships, and tooting trains to see the world, or simply to visit relatives. And when Auntie and the cousins arrived, it was often for a long stay. Making relatives part of the household is still a pleasure: In an old family house, a well-furnished room, with an heirloom bed and hand-knit coverlet, need never update its welcome—everyone would object if it did. An 1860's painted screen, left, glamorously recalls the great-grandparents' trip to Italy.

"Her art sisters the natural roses."

—SHAKESPEARE

Even a city bedroom can be a guest-garden when sprightly botanical images communicate the hostess's passion for plants. Prints, on a duvet and framed over the bed, opposite, recall early botanical studies published in Renaissance "florilegia"—volumes of scientific drawings of plants showing root, stem, leaf, and blossom in precise detail. It's a challenge artists delight in taking up to this day. But then, flowers were ever a favorite bed-chamber motif—an evocation of freshness and youth, perhaps, or a secret wish to sleep in a bed strewn with petals, whatever the season. Although Mary, Queen of Scots, had bed hangings embroidered with "potts of floures" in cloth of silver and gold, guests will probably find a pillowcase embroidered with wildflowers, right, petals enough to lay a cheek on.

A self-contained little cottage at the end of the garden or just beyond the pool is a wonderful way to provide privacy for guests and hosts alike. For starts, no early-rising visitor has to tiptoe into the kitchen for coffee if the cottage is equipped with breakfast supplies and a minimum of kitchen conveniences. And when the hideaway is cozily and cheerfully decorated, what guests wouldn't love tucking in for an après-ski nap or a rainy-day read? A room-wide cotton plaid rug invites them to pad about barefoot even in winter—and there's plenty of extra firewood stacked on the porch. Here the same blue-and-white toile pattern on wallpaper, bed, and sofa lends unity and sophistication to an all-in-one room. But be warned: You may just have to pry your guests out of their enchanted retreat to visit with them at all.

To show high regard for a guest, give her a castle of a bed that requires a stool to climb into, above. The sturdy headboard recalls Victorian millwork, yet an original would surely have been of somber dark wood—not this contemporary lightness of satiny cream. Letting the same hue theme the entire room helps heavy pieces to float.

Opposite: For intrepid British colonists, life in alien climes was a curious mixture of adaptability and civility. In India, Jamaica, or Africa, how cheering it was to have guests from "Home"—perhaps a young niece or nephew seeking opportunity, adventure, or romance. At a plantation on the Caribbean island of Nevis, locally crafted mahogany beds

adopted familiar European forms. Though the Oriental rugs were no doubt packed for the long voyage along with the silver and table linens, simple cottons cool the bed, and shutters block the noonday heat while letting in the trade winds. It's a clean, fine look admired today—stripped of fussiness and yet somehow forever England.

"The happiest part of a man's life is what he passes lying awake in bed in the morning."

SAMUEL JOHNSON

Do you remember the joy of opening your first really big box of colored crayons? Here, in a cottage in the French countryside, lives a grownup who never forgot it. With cherry walls and sunny yellow to lift the low ceiling, she inexpensively created a guest room in an ancient house by indulging a passion for hues as bright as gumdrops, proving you can still color the world happy. More life comes from casually imitating a classically French **lit à poloniase** *that drapes the bed in merry candy-stripes. "When you paint a piece in bright colors, it becomes a toy for the imagination," says the owner, who likes to keep on adding things to a room—like the faded canvas camp chair—until it "begins to tell the story of everyday life." In such a scheme—spirited, uninhibited, and fun—colors and prints that don't "match" do suit the mood, expressing just how she and her company feel about escaping Paris at the end of the week and kicking off their shoes in the country.*

The Children's Room

Y ou remember the wallpaper, and the faces and figures you saw hidden in the pattern. You built a theater in the corner with toys that became real and had lives and stories. You bounced wildly on the bed and hurled pillows at your intruding brother. When you had a cold, your doll had one, too, and got half the pillow.

A child's room is a world—incalculable what goes on there. Parents who lovingly decorate the nursery before a first-born arrives, who later sensitively calibrate the timing for a first "big-boy bed," are both remembering and shaping, for they hold a vision for their child that smiles from each night-light and quilt and bunny. Security and gladness are its keynotes, whatever its sunny colors. And as a cradle gives way to a crib, and the crib to a child bed (which the child invariably tumbles out of with an alarming midnight thud), the youngster's own personality begins subtley to shape the space. The Bear Without Whom Sleep Is Impossible is abandoned for a scatter of coloring and picture books, and a miniature wardrobe for every possible glamorous event in a doll's life. He spends hours looping race-car tracks across the entire floor; she putters with clay and busily neglects to pick up.

In those precious years when parents can have their say, creating a child's bedroom is an act of love and imagination, a way to stimulate a nascent spirit with color and charm. With every crib mobile and cheerful curtain we hang, we pray them sweet dreams, knowing that, even for infants, their dreams are their own.

However adventurous a little one is by day—wandering off or climbing to the top of the slide—he wants an enclosed world at night. This painted bed cradles a sleeper, while toys rest on high. Tomorrow, when sunlight pokes through curtains of circus-tent stripes, he'll want to go down that slide head-first!

"In the corner of the bedroom is a great big curtain.
Someone lives behind it but I don't know who."

A.A. MILNE

Is there a child alive who doesn't love a tent? A fortunate youngster whose mother has canopied and curtained her bed in red checks, opposite, has no need to drape a tablecloth over two chairs to know the sweet secrecy a play tent provides. She's a princess, a bedouin, a ship captain setting sail with two bears for crew, and all within the comforting realm of her own pillow and mattress. When a cotton fabric is as classically happy (and washable) as this one, think of using it in quantity. Then, just possibly, that moment when it's time for bed will be smooth sailing. Sweet as new cream from the top of the bottle, a pristine bed with its pale carvings, right, will last a lass from "Winnie-the-Pooh" through "Wuthering Heights." With apricot walls bearing the poet's laurel crown, who knows what words of her own will come of it all one day?

An age arrives when a changing
child wants nothing changed. You
may not remove the miniature wing
chair because it has always been
there; and Bear, too, and the barn
with its little horses asleep inside.
Though he's already hitting base
runs and his sleep-over pals tend to
somersault through the pillows, his
sunny ground-floor bedroom, with
its familiar play of red and blue
stripes, is just the way he wants it.
A bed without headboard or
footboard can make the room seem
more open, softer. Toys can be stored
under the long window seat, where
sunlight picks out Mom's greeting
on a "good-morning" pillow, above.

"The children's eye is forever being educated, and ugly things ought not to be brought superfluously before them."

— CLARENCE COOK

Long ago a mother on a Swedish farm lined and dressed a cradle, opposite, stitching its bonnet and gathered skirt by hand. Practical handles made it easy for her to keep her baby close by as she worked in the kitchen and weeded the garden. Now she has seen her grandbabies laughing up at her from the same cradle, a family treasure in a small historic house on the coast of Sweden. But as these children grew, the house didn't. The solution was to nestle a girl's bed into a cozy alcove under the eaves, cutting a window not much bigger than a porthole to the sun. It's a berth both snug and snuggly, where a child can sleep with angels, handpainted on her special quilt.

THE CRIB

It seems eons before that snoozy newborn, at sea in the vast crib, becomes a bouncy, upright character grabbing at the bars and threatening to tumble over them into the world. (Or is it only minutes, hours?) Though infants have slept tidily in bureau drawers and parents' beds, they graduated only recently from traditional cradles to the bumpered safety of a modern crib. A little world, decorated to both soothe and stimulate, the crib becomes an arena of discovery, where heels kick, lullabies comfort, and from which, eventually, bottles and toys are hurled forth with rambunctious glee.

Oh, to be a little girl again, if only to wake into one's own fantasy room! Branches of birch make curtain rods shaped by nature, looped like a ball gown with waves and cascades of airy net. "I want a tree," she told her mother, and there it arches, growing from the corner, branching across the ceiling to shelter her bed. "With cherries," she added as an afterthought; and so the kind muralist painted cherries. Against all-white furnishings, wide golden stripes painted on the wall lend definition to a corner room in a renovated Californa bungalow. Pink and yellow, a tricky combination rarely tried, make happy bedfellows here, where pink is all in the accents, such as the rosy botanical print that dances boldly on the quilt and pillows. The perfect tiered table for rounding off the play corner was originally a plant stand, found in a garden shop.

Gentle Asides

"Come put up your feet and sit a while" is a time-honored greeting among country people. Typically, it says a lot in a little: "You must be tired" and, "You can relax here—you don't have to sit proper with your feet on the floor." Sitting proper has its place, of course, but so has the ancient, easeful art of reclining. A daybed plumped with pillows, a chaise longue with a cuddly throw, and even an out-of-the-way window seat invite a torporous, slightly unbuttoned comfort we associate with true relaxation. It's a state that earlier, less puritanical, cultures knew all about. Whether you reclined to dine on a Greek or Roman couch, or lounged back upon your host's sumptuous rugs and pillows in Turkey or India, your welcome was often a stretched-out one. In 18th-century France, the private boudoir of a lady of leisure would certainly have contained a coquettish chaise lounge (literally, "long chair"), a furnishing whose most famous rendering in art was Goya's overtly sensuous painting, the Naked Maja. The *recamier*, a version with a curving back, is named for a French socialite of the same period, Madame Recamier, whose salon drew some of Paris's most brilliant and beautiful. What's in a name? Often volumes of social change, for in the world of the more straight-laced (and often unhealthily corsetted) Victorians, this comfortable half-sofa became known as a fainting couch.

Though we are less prone to fainting spells today, we are admittedly sometimes drowsy as we curl up with a book on a window seat; and sometimes the

> *Late afternoon: The low point of the day becomes a high point if we can take time for a cup of tea. Its very fragrance rinses the mind. On a porch chaise clad in a glad lilac print, there is every excuse to drowse a bit, then rise again, renewed.*

We all have a need for nooks that a window seat, opposite, wonderfully satisfies. Almost in the garden, barely in the room, it is a retreat, an observer's post, that invites contemplation. The pulled-back drapes not only suggest a certain theatricality, but offer a secret place any child playing hide-and-seek would immediately head for. In an entryway or bay, as a pause on the landing of a grand staircase, or as a bedroom bower, a window seat pulls the window wall into the room's comforts. And practically speaking, if vented at the bottom, it's a great way to cover up a radiator.

Spare and elegant, a guest chamber in a historic building in Ireland, right, was designed by Sybil Connolly, a multifaceted designer and champion of Irish craftsmanship. Were it not for its fine, black-edged curves, the daybed would all but melt into the wall. Why toile in Ireland, a fabric associated with France? "Believe it or not," says Connolly, "toile was invented by a man who lived near Dublin."

book loses out. But like children who can try every position but the right one in a big, soft chair, and who often prefer to read flat out on the floor, we cannot resist the invitation to be supine. Whether we prop our legs on an ottoman in the living room or stretch out on a sofa-like daybed that converts to a real bed at night, we have found a hospitable inclination, half-bed, half-chair. Having such gentle asides tucked about the house adds a restful, welcoming look, as if these "put-up-your-feet" corners could at any moment give something of a bedroom's blessing. And, at the drop of an eyelid, they can.

A PASSEL OF PILLOWS

Although Jacob in the Bible laid his head upon a stone and dreamed
of angels, we prefer pillows that are a touch of heaven themselves,
soothing gravity's tug on neck and back with the softness of a
cloud. From early times, pillows and bolsters covered with luxurious
fabrics have spoken of hospitality—whether scattered on rugs
and couches or piled as a welcome on a visitor's bed. When planning
a room's menu, think of pillows as tasty little hors d'oeuvres—
whipped up from elegant ingredients such as lace, silk, and fringe,
spiced with variety, and presented in inviting arrays. To guarantee
sweet sleep, tuck a sachet of soporific herbs such as lavender, rose
petals, woodruff, or Our Lady's bedstraw into the pillowcase.

Harmony or diversity—play pillows
either way. On a snowy window seat,
above, pillows of graded sizes extend
a gentle invitation, each mauve or
white puff sporting distinctive
details. Plumped with softness on
three sides, this tented bed with
matching sheets and shams is a
haven of serenity, opposite. Though
not a day bed, it becomes one,
lending a single room some of the
grandeur of a suite.

One of the most endearing elements of Victorian houses is the windowed bay, above, crowning sometimes dark rooms with a bow of light. Not only a focal point but the place where everyone wants to relax and look out, a bay can be tricky to decorate. The updated solution here is a low-sided daybed so lightly sketched in metal that it does not intrude on the fine woodwork of the windows. Or call it a summery, double-ended chaise—just the place to swing up bare legs for an hour of reading while the sprinkler swishes on the lawn outside. And surely any tired child objecting to a nap could be coaxed to take one with the promise that she can curl up in this restful corner. Opposite: No collector of antique laces wants to keep all her prizes tucked away where she can't enjoy them. In a spare bedroom, drapes, bed, pillows, and stool have been dressed and fringed in handmade finery found on trips to England and France. The most frequent guest? The collector herself, who admits she escapes to this room to do her planning, surrounded by the airiest of arts.

"I wish the sky would rain down roses . . . it would be like sleeping and yet waking all at once."

GEORGE ELIOT

Sofas are so traditionally part of our lives that we often forget that other shapes and easeful arrangements can provide both comparable comfort and decorative dash. A living-room corner, opposite, is a flower-lover's haven, where old-fashioned rose paintings have been echoed by a gathering of floral pillows in tapestry, needlepoint, and transferred photography. Yet this composed garden began with but an iron bench and a simple, duck-covered mattress. And who wouldn't love to settle into a squishy, pillowed chair, right, and put up weary feet on a matching ottoman? Rosy and ruffled (note the friendly use of three complementary fabrics), this grandma chair is the ultimate seduction, as cozy in the bedroom as in a living room, family room, or study.

At Beauty's Table

What little girl has not been drawn to the mysteries of her mother's dressing table? For in that corner of the bedroom lies magic—feminine alchemy—created of pale potions in crystal vials, gold tubes for ruby lips, fat puffs of powder, tiny flacons that uncork a dizzying fragrance. Everything begs to be touched, tried, smelled—and sooner or later, alas, most little ladies find the invitation irresistible.

But for grown-ups, the dressing table (also aptly named a "vanity") is a place of quiet preparation and appraising self-regard. There are regimens. (Remember brushing your hair 100 strokes daily to give it shine?) There is confrontation—fatigued eyes or pale cheeks to tint with a fingertip of artifice. In the private moments spent at our dressing table, whether brief or languorous, we can experiment—tug back a lock to imagine ourselves with shorter or curlier hair, decide which earrings best suit the outfit.

Lifting a string of pearls from their case, it's comforting to remember how ancient an instinct we act on. Many primitive tribes wore only jewelry, which often had magical properties. Fashionable Egyptians etched their eyes with a cream made from crushed ant's eggs, and Queen Nefertiti painted her fingernails a royal red. Cleopatra blackened her eyebrows with kohl; Greek courtesans scented their breath; and Roman ladies shadowed their eyes with saffron. Little kohl pots and flasks recovered from the ancient past indicate that women have long devoted themselves to their image, perhaps assisted by attendants or

Under the eye of the mirror, beauty's handmaiden and truth-teller, the dressing table is surely a woman's most personal arena. Indulging the senses with beautiful glass flasks or antique accessories only adds to a bedroom's message of intimacy.

Lace, crystal, silver, porcelain—no material was too precious for the fashionable dressing table of the last century, when a display of fine ornament attested to a family's status. Even in Russia, a visitor in 1803 reported, her guest room held a silver and silver-gilt toilet set, a traditional part of a Russian bride's dowry and always of the most precious metal her family could afford. Many of these feminine luxuries, such as the round powder pot, opposite, or a set of silver-topped jars on their own tray, are still found in antiques shops today and make collectibles that are a joy to use. Although a claw-footed mahogany pedestal table like this one might be expected to grace a library, it serves its lady beautifully with the addition of a freestanding mirror, lacy lampshades, and a damask-covered stool in shell pink. For those who love the gleam of wood, a bureau top, left, with interesting boxes and cases may be all that's needed to organize a few assists to grooming.

peering into polished metal long before glass mirrors became available in the 1600s. On braiding, curling, rolling, and coloring hair alone, women have lavished hours of their lives. But none were so burdened as Louis XV's court ladies, who staggered under three-foot upsweeps adorned with birdcages or ship models!

As we prepare ourselves to face the world, we, too, are playing an artful game attuned to fashion and fantasy, as well as to the demands of our own work and style. And if a glance in the mirror fails to reveal a handsome hero standing at our shoulder with a diamond necklace in his adoring hands, no matter; there are greater rewards: those moments when the woman in the mirror looks back with happiness, self-knowledge, and acceptance.

The convenience of having not just a dressing table, but an actual dressing room is so appealing that today's architects have increasingly included such a space within modern master bedroom suites. Here, a dressing nook has been created in an older house, separate but adjoining the bedroom, where a woman can claim her own space for the comforts that bring her fresh to the day. A cotton-skirted table edged with lace suffices for a vanity—one could soften an old dresser or chest similarly, leaving the hidden drawers for storage. After she bathes, there's a slip-covered divan to curl up in as she dries her hair, far more relaxing an invitation to linger than a stiff vanity chair. Instead of filmy curtains, the vintage lingerie she displays on a coatrack picks up the walls' peachy glow—a color, by the way, that is particularly complimentary to complexions.

"There were treasures on Mother's dressing table . . . a Wedgewood pin dish, a little porcelain Mary and her lamb, the pale green, flowered top of a rose bowl that had broken, and Mother's silver-backed comb and brush and mirror. All these held meaning for me. Each was—and still is—capable of evoking a rush of memories." So wrote the anthropologist Margaret Mead, recalling her childhood in "Blackberry Winter." When we are lucky enough to inherit such personal keepsakes from a mother or grandmother, the dressing table holds a special intimacy of feeling that links woman to woman. For beauty's little rituals, think of choosing a piece of furniture you would welcome into the bedroom's mix in any case, such as a small table, opposite, painted to match the wall and wainscotting. A folk-art cupboard, with its pretty lace backdrop, takes cosmetics; when they're shut away, you have a writing desk. With its top down, a Windsor-style desk becomes a vanity with a sense of tradition, from silver catch-all tray to antique silver picture frames, above. The look is fine without frill, save for tiny rosebuds skirting the lampshades.

*"Here first she bathes, and round her body pours
Soft oils of fragrance and ambrosial showers."*

—HOMER

Jewelry that matters, the kind one imagines a granddaughter wearing one day, should be kept free of scratches and tangles. Although tissue serves well, cases lined with soft, silky fabric, left, are ideal for protecting jewelry, particularly when they have inner compartments that keep precious pieces separate. Our great-grandmothers, who expected to own and preserve their finery for a lifetime at least, often had drawers filled with such supple, beribboned cases, perhaps handmade by a sister as a bridal gift, like the lace-trimmed one with the tassle. A flat case such as this might hold lace hankies, collars, or silk hose, all neatly folded away and safe from snags. If toiletries tend to accumulate on the bathroom sink, solve the clutter problem by making it lovely clutter, opposite, transferring lotions and soaps to antique containers sure to greet your morning with a gleam.

Layers of Luxury

PART FOUR

Linens and Laces

We wear our bed next to our skin—reason enough for the bedroom to be the most tactile and sensuous of all rooms. Stretching between fresh sheets, pulling a plump duvet up to our chins, we are wrapped in the caress of smooth fabrics that wick away care and weariness. Weave becomes warmth; softness cocoons sleep. Even making the bed each morning—a tedious task to a hurried teenager—brings quiet satisfaction to an adult. The mere act of smoothing the sheets and straightening the spread, perhaps propping a lace-edged pillow just so, is a kind of loving thank-you to a dear friend.

Though some of the most sublime textiles the world has known have been lavished on the bed, from handwoven tapestries and embroidered silks to satin sheets (French courtesans favored black ones, to emphasize their pale complexions), none has proved more gently satisfying than linen, the oldest fabric woven by man. Linen fragments over 3500 years old have been recovered from Egyptian tombs, and its luxury made it the preferred choice for the robes of priests and emperors throughout the ancient world. Until the industrial revolution, most families cut, hemmed, and embroidered their bed linens at home, and girls slowly filled their hope chests with their own skilled work. Affluent Victorian brides, however, might stop in Paris or Brussels on their honeymoon tour to order up monogrammed linens for a lifetime—sometimes 20 pairs of bedsheets, as well as sumptuous tablecloths, napkins, and towels. Over years of laundering, such sheets grow only softer, and,

Couples need not tussle for a favorite pillow when one's own is so sweetly and discreetly labeled. Even those who eschew the formality of monograms might delight in such a wedding or anniversary gift, especially when the ground of the claim is fine linen.

Since the Italians refined lace-making in the 1500s, inviting air and light into the pattern of openwork stitches, variations of the art passed from country to country, but have never passed out of fashion. Such was the appetite for lace among gentlemen as well as ladies of the 1600s that some countries passed sumptuary laws prohibiting all but the highest classes to wear this badge of luxury. Cascades of it adorned French bedrooms during the Second Empire, and Victorian brides rippled with lace from veil to train. Antique needle-lace panels found in Europe, opposite, perhaps once used at the window, soften a contemporary bed of wrought iron, as, on the table, a layer of lace available by the yard echoes their ivory glow. Smaller pieces, left, can find renewed life as trim for shams, pillows, and bolsters. This clever collector has edged new linen sheets with antique **pointe de Venise.**

remarkably, many escaped the scorch marks of maids' irons to be usable today.

Even more than fine bed linens, lace was always a treasure for show. Its angelic delicacy has long made lace a natural attendant of the feminine body and bedchamber; but with the advent of machine-made lace in the 19th century, the many, and not just the few, could afford a flutter of finery at the window, a lace-and-linen counterpane, or airily ornamental panels drifting from high bedposts. For us, there is more than nostalgia in cherishing such fine fabrics today. For the eye, too, is a sensualist, drawing its sustenance from beauty.

To a contemporary bedroom that's as serene as a beach at dawn, a touch of white lace brings a welcome variation of texture, a hint of pattern. Readily available cotton panels at the door, opposite, have a crisp clarity of design, and stand up well to laundering. (Note the palm-frond motif woven into them—an 18th-century symbol of sleep.) Filmier drifts of Scottish lace barely brush the bed, which is dressed in pure white linen from headboard to summer coverlet. Though ancient companions in luxury, linen and lace can be as fresh and classic as the furnishings here, all reproduction Swedish Gustavian pieces, including a charming little footstool, right. One can imagine children bursting into such a room to bounce their parents awake; then, to justify the racket, sweetly presenting their gift of wildflowers.

ADAPTABLE FOOTSTOOLS

A blessing to readers and tired feet, footstools were long associated with the elderly. But youngsters may love these portable perches even more—so easy to maneuver into position to reach the cookie jar! "My children stand on it when they brush their teeth," admits the designer of this one. Comfortably pillowed, a footstool becomes an extra seat when not another chair could possibly wedge itself into the social circle around the fire. Then again, you could put your feet up on it.

Layering a bed for comfort is rather like building a complex pastry. Few of us would give up modern box springs and mattresses, but those made with horsehair still have an enduring quality. Next we want a mattress pad (quilted cotton, fleece, or even wool) to insulate us from mattress bumps. If you love the finished look of a bedskirt, like the gathered lace one opposite, it will not shift if attached to a fitted sheet over the box spring. We tend to choose our cotton sheets for their color or pattern, but keep in mind that the most luxurious are percale, with a thread count of 200 or above. Cotton or linen blanket covers, once **de rigueur** to protect the sleeper from itchy wool, are still a lovely choice: a fine antique linen one could also serve as a summer coverlet. And the down-filled duvet, like a buttery mound of frosting on top, is a European custom Americans have adopted with a passion—sometimes simplifying all bedding to only a sheet and it!

So many appealing, good-quality bed linens are available today that shopping for the bed can be deliriously confusing. Sometimes the result is a dizzy linen closet piled with conflicting colors and patterns. One way to harmonize your choices is to start with a single, best-beloved piece, and build the bedding from there. In the room on these pages, the inspiration is a family treasure: a white quilt appliqued with delicate pink flowers and a large bow. Not only its colors, but its mood of crisp innocence led the owner's eye to several compatible patterns, each subtle, each balancing the rose of the quilt's flowers with lots of white. The pillows above make a happy family, from a classic ticking pattern, to a more delicate ribbon stripe, to an actual embroidered ribbon trimming the bolster. The effect is not at all flowery, though pale flowers fleck the sheets. Another good idea when investing in a well-dressed bed: Buy two sets of sheets and pillowcases in your pattern, or a set in each of two patterns that will dovetail as nicely as these. The result is a room thought out carefully from the start—including the ceiling border opposite and vanity skirt above—that any decorator would be proud of.

STORING LINENS

Enjoy cherished linens by stocking them in plain sight.

There is something so abundantly satisfying about what poet Rupert Brooke called "the cool kindliness" of smooth, freshly laundered bed linens that it seems a shame to shut them away in a closet. If the collection is a fine one—such as woven cotton coverlets and lace-edged linen shams—displaying them on open, lace-trimmed shelves is just as decorative as displaying good china. And since damp is an enemy, linens do better where fresh air circulates. A few storage tips: Try to keep folded linens out of direct sunlight, and unfold and use them frequently enough so that crease-marks don't set or discolor.

Bed linens "white as snow and sweet as a rose" were as much the pride of a well-run household in the 1700s and 1800s as they are now. Before the liberation of washing machines, however, it's a wonder home laundresses, much less the linens themselves, survived the rigors of wash day. Weekly, as copper pots were set to boiling, family linens were soaked, washed in homemade soap, boiled, stirred, scoured, bleached, rinsed, and wrung. For an extra whiteness and sweetening, linens might be laid out on the grass in the sun, but taken in before the dew. Ideally they dried sailing in the breeze on a clothesline (and how ideal it still is!), but in inclement weather a week's sodden wash would have to be hung before the kitchen fire or strung across the attic. For whitening antique linens, some of the old remedies are still good: scrubbing, lemon juice, baking soda, and, yes, sunlight.

A great gust of fresh air blew into
American bedrooms in the early
1900s on a wave of concern for
health and hygiene. Windows were
flung open, dust-collecting drapes
and hangings pulled down, and
maids set to rigorous regimens of
scouring. The pristine look of a
seemingly timeless room reminds us
that purity does not mean lack of
comfort. The simple iron bed (not
unlike Franklin Delano Roosevelt's
childhood bed at Hyde Park, his
family home) is crisp with layered
cottons topped by a Marseilles
spread. There's a tufted love seat to
curl up on, and, to fortify one's
nights against those chill (but oh,
so healthy) winter breezes, there's
always a fluffy wool blanket to pull
up to one's ears, leaving only a cold
nose exposed.

In this day of synthetics and computer-born patterns, it's amazing to think how many of the fabrics that most strongly appeal to our senses had their origin in antique lands. Damask, for example, whose subtle patterns are woven in one or two colors, with warp and weft contrasting, takes its name from Damascus, an ancient center of the silk trade. Glistening white damask cloths were as proudly displayed on princely dining tables of the 16th century as they are at festive occasions today—and fortunate is the home that inherits heavy linen damask napkins to match! Whether in linen, cotton, or a blend of the two, damask has long graced the bed with a lustrous look that is richer, quieter (and often sturdier) than a simple print, its texture a ripple of pattern that catches and tosses the light. Though white and ivory damask are surely the favorites of the ages, two-toned hues of toast or other soft colors lend a bedroom a special glow, gently bridging present and past.

Cream, coffee, and toast—think of them as one casual color played in varying shades of restfulness. A daisy-chain stitched on net filters the morning light, left. Used en suite, a small-figured cotton damask trimmed with bright white suggests both simplicity and opulence. The same material used on bolster, shams, and duvet cover frames a droll march of bone buttons on the oblong pillow.

Cheered with chintz and a vintage quilt, a small bedroom feels as cozy as a teapot. One can't help imagining a cottage garden tangled with roses just outside these windows, which are crowned with rumpled swags knotted like big buds at the ends. Though we think of chintz as quintessentially English, the gaily printed cotton fabric first came to England's shores from India in the 1700s and was immediately all the rage. Of course the resourceful English soon learned to print their own chintz, making its gay floral patterns forever their own. The demure print used here, with its softly "faded" background, evokes highly prized vintage Victorian chintzes.

Stitches in Time

From cottages to palaces, few little girls of the past escaped rigorous tutelage and hours of practice in the needle arts. Think of those generations of little heads bent to their work by the fireplace, striving for stitches regular and tiny and strong! For upon their skill as women would depend the ornamenting of the household, and often, its warmth and comfort as well. From lace, intricate embroidery, and crochet work, to applique, quilting, trapunto, pettipoint, dressmaking, and plain old mending—the styles they mastered depended on their culture and time. Yet when it came to fancy work, each put something of herself, a touch of imagination and delight, into the traditional figures that flowed from her fingers.

A special sentiment has always gone into the making of bed clothes and, particularly, coverlets. For with every dip of the needle, the creator can't help but blend her prayer for the sleeper's enduring love, warmth, and health. A century and a half ago, had you visited a tiny Provençal village clamped on a mountainside, a stately English mansion, or a hardscrabble New Hampshire farm, you would have seen beauty on the bed and felt the pride in it.

Fortunately for us, many of those patient stitches have survived the years, to warm our own nights. And they still inspire styles and skills that engage our artistry and relax the mind: There's a unique pleasure in making something beautiful. For those who still know how to speak their love with needle and thread, the tradition goes on, connecting the heart, the hand, and the generations.

Not the glamour of the fabric but the working of it distinguishes this closely quilted trapunto spread made in England, its flowers raised in relief by inserted stuffing. Restrained it seems, until light picks out the exuberant design.

Layers equal warmth, and a quilt is essentially just that—two outer layers sandwiching a third, possibly of soft cotton or wool batting, the whole securely bonded with stitching. Yet if that's the scale, what a variety of tunes it can play! These antique quilts from Wales, made for rural homes, reveal a passion for colorful, printed chintzes, which are overlaid with yet more pattern. The swirled and criss-crossed stitching was not the work of housewives but of itinerant quilters who sewed up the fabric supplied. Long overlooked as antiques, these quilts are now prized for their homey charm.

Every bed bears a message, though not always in words. Only you who dress it know what it's saying, of what consolations and memories it murmurs. On the first frosty night of autumn—the one that will surely do in the garden—it's time to unfold an heirloom quilt, opposite, and delight again in its hopeful message of bright rosebuds appliqued over puffy cotton. And as if that poignancy were not enough, delicately embroidered pillow shams, above, make clear in words the seasons that have, and will, transpire. For embroidery to slide from word to picture and back again is only natural, since every child's first embroidery lesson was once an alphabet sampler. The paired verses opposite—"Sweet lilies close their eyes at night / And open with the morning light"—charmingly tie our rhythms to nature's. Their delicate leaves seem sketched by a deft pencil—a very contemporary, and easy, style for a beginning embroiderer to emulate.

A CALENDAR
from
One Friend
to Another
1918

On the cross-hatch of canvas,
what glorious needlepoint images
have flowered—from bold designs
to shadings as subtle as those of
an oil painting. Though tapestry,
a close cousin, is woven on great
looms, a needlepoint frame could
be taken up by a woman at any
time. Of course she made
pillows—a welcome comfort to
hard 18th-century chairs—but
also bench covers and even
pictures for the wall. Also called
"Berlin work," for the town
that gave birth to complete
needlepoint kits, this is an art so
enduring that each generation
seems to discover it anew.

MONOGRAMS

This ancient art reaches far back into castle cupboards of the Renaissance.

For generations, brides have felt a special thrill in seeing their own initials stitched decoratively on pillow cases, bed sheets, and guest towels. During the Renaissance, the handwoven linens in a noble bride's dowry—a precious part of the wealth she brought to marriage—were monogrammed with her coat of arms for purposes of identification. The fashionable upper classes took up the custom in the 18th century, and, lacking hereditary emblems, set their initials—always in white—amid elegantly embroidered designs. It was not until the 1920s that monograms in delicate colors were introduced by the venerable Paris firm of D. Portault. Among the notables who turned to their expert hand embroiderers was Princess Grace of Monaco, who had her linens monogrammed with her favorite flower—a blue hydrangea.

Scents

Smell is a sense so deeply attached to memory that the fragrance of a certain soap can vividly recall the presence of a beloved grandmother; a whiff of lilacs can transport us to a long-ago moment of childhood. As much as color and texture, fragrance is a mood-setter: Think of the excitement stirred by the piney spice of Christmas boughs, or the soothing aroma of a minted tea as we settle into bed for an hour of reading. No doubt our primitive ancestors relied on their noses, as animals do, to tell them what foods were good and where fresh water ran; and often we still turn toward pleasure nose-first.

Surely nothing concocted or bottled can ever equal the smell of clean sheets that have dried outdoors, snaring wind and sun in their weave to be released later, like a blown kiss, to the sleeper. Linen cloths starched and ironed add their own suggestion of scrubbed tradition to the air. To these base notes, we add overtones entirely personal, as intimate as lingerie that has been folded away with a rose-petal sachet, or the hint of a favorite perfume lingering like a signature in air. In spring, when the daffodils finally bloom, who can resist placing just a few in a vase by the bed, to waft their ineffable message of hope to our dreams?

To defeat winter's dry indoor heat, water a potted plant by the bedroom window; the smell of damp soil and grateful leaves brings a momentary gust of the tropics. Instinctively, we find our own ways to make a bedroom smell as good as it looks. For to sweeten our place of sleep with nature's balms is simply in our nature.

Just as the scent of leather, furniture polish, and old books evokes the study, a laundered freshness, sweet as a June meadow, is the keynote of a well-loved bedroom. Here, a rose and potted lavender bring spring's sprightly fragrance indoors.

For a traveler who must try to feel
at home in one impersonal hotel
room after another, a scented
candle in its own silver traveling
case, opposite, along with a fold-up
triptych of family photos, can make
all the difference between feeling
lonely and settling in quite cozily.
To help a houseguest feel even more
at home, wrap up a subtle blend of
dried potpourri in a bundle of fresh
leaves, right, and add a blossoming
bunch of lilacs; when the flowers
fade, the guest will still have a
lasting little gift to take home to
remember her visit by.

When the last of the garden's flowers bow out and the scent of damp autumn leaves wafts into the bedroom, it seems there's nothing left to fill a vase with. This is the time for a more scintillating menu of indoor fragrances, such as eucalyptus leaves tied with berries, right, a wreath of dried herbs, or an orangey-cinnamon potpourri in an open bowl. And why wait until Christmas to savor the snap of bristling spruce boughs? By the bedroom hearth, save the sweetest-burning logs of all: hickory and apple-wood. Then, in the depth of winter, you might splurge on florists' roses, letting their summery notes float in from an old-fashioned washstand, opposite.

Our greatest luxury is one we pay little heed to: the ability to command a gush of fresh water with the twist of a faucet. Only when a plumbing failure leaves us high and dry can we appreciate how arduous it was to keep a household smelling fresh when water had to be toted or pumped. In the days between ritual Saturday night baths, many adults washed up from a pitcher and bowl on the bedroom commode, while at the kitchen sink children were scoured as briskly as pots.

To sweeten the home, floral and herbal fragrances have been valued for centuries. Frankincense, for example, a gift of the Wise Men, was a tree gum prized for its fragrance throughout the Middle East. And though strewing rose petals upon sheets sounds utterly romantic, it once had the urgency of necessity. While our lives now are simplified and purified by abundant water, nature's subtle fragrances remain a precious gift.

Photography